W9-AZX-525

STECK-VAUGHN

# WINNERS

## OLYMPIC GAMES

Melissa Stone Billings

Henry Billings

STECK-VAUGHN®
C O M P A N Y
A Subsidiary of National Education Corporation

**Books in this series:**

Congressional Medal of Honor
Halls of Fame
**Olympic Games**
Nobel Prize

## Acknowledgments

**Executive Editor**

Elizabeth Strauss

**Photo Editor**

Margie Foster

**Production and Design**

Howard Adkins Communications

**Cover Illustration**

Linda Adkins Design

**Photo Credits**

P.2 AP/Wide World; p.3 AP/Wide World; p.5 AP/Wide World; p.7 UPI/Bettmann; p.10 UPI/Bettmann; p.11 UPI/Bettmann; p.13 UPI/Bettmann; p.16 © Eric Schweikardt/Sports Illustrated; p.17 AP/Wide World; p.19 © John Zimmerman/Sports Illustrated; p.22 © James Drake/Sports Illustrated; p.23 UPI/Bettmann; p.25 AP/Wide World; p.28 AP/Wide World; p.29 AP/Wide World; p.30 © Jerry Cooke/Sports Illustrated; p.34 © Focus On Sports; p.35 © Focus On Sports; p.36 © Tony Duffy/Allsport; p.39 © Allsport; p.42 © Focus On Sports; p.43 © Manny Millan/Sports Illustrated; p.45 © Focus On Sports; p.46 © Focus On Sports; p.50 © Mike Powell/Allsport; p.51 © Manny Millan/Sports Illustrated; p.52 © Bob Martin/Allsport; p.55 © Richard Mackson/Focus On Sports; p.58 © Tony Duffy/Allsport; p.59 © Focus On Sports; p.60 © Tony Duffy/Allsport; p.62 © Mike Powell/Allsport; p.66 AP/Wide World; p.67 © Peter Read Miller/Sports Illustrated; p.69 © Simon Bruty/Allsport; p.72 © Focus On Sports; p.73 © Tony Duffy/Allsport; p.75 © John McDonough/Sports Illustrated; p.77 © John Biever/Sports Illustrated; p.80 © Richard Martin/Allsport; p.81 © Focus On Sports; p.83 © Heinz Kluetmeier/Sports Illustrated.

**ISBN 0-8114-4784–7**

2 3 4 5 6 7 8 9 0 PO 97 96 95 94

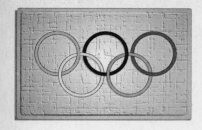

# The Olympic Games

The Olympic games were first held in Greece about 3,000 years ago. They were meant to honor the Greek gods. At first, the athletes simply ran foot races. Slowly the games developed to include others sports such as wrestling, spear throwing, and chariot racing. Then, in 394 A.D., a Roman emperor ended the games.

In 1896, the Olympic games began again in Athens, Greece. Since then, the Olympics have moved from one world city to another every four years. The games now include such different sports as gymnastics, ice skating, diving, and skiing. The winner of each event receives a gold medal.

## Contents

# Sammy Lee

## Diving for Gold

"*P*op, guess what?" shouted Sammy Lee as he burst into the kitchen one day in 1933. "I've found it!"

"Found what?" asked his father.

"I've found my sport!" cried Sammy. "I just did a one-and-a-half **somersault** dive. And now I know what I'm going to be. I'm going to be an Olympic diver!"

The next day, Mr. Lee went and watched his son dive. "Sammy," said Mr. Lee quietly, "you can be anything you want . . . after you become a doctor."

## Olympic Dreams

When Sammy was twelve years old, the 1932 Summer Olympic Games were held in Los Angeles. Sammy wanted to go, but the ticket prices were too high. His father told him how the world's best **athletes** meet in one place every four years. Sammy learned that they **compete** for medals and **glory**, not for money. "Pop," Sammy said, "some day I want to be an Olympic champion."

Mr. Lee laughed to himself. "Well, in what sport?" he asked Sammy.

"Gee, I don't know, Pop," Sammy answered. "But some day I'll find it."

Sammy Lee found his sport at a city pool in Los Angeles. He was doing somersaults off the diving board when a friend suggested he try something harder. Boldly Sammy tried a one-and-a-half

**athletes**
people who are trained in exercises or sports

**compete**
try to win by beating others

**glory**
honor and praise

Sammy Lee diving in 1948 Olympic trials

3

talent
skill

somersault. As soon as he did it, he knew he had discovered his true **talent**. He later said, "Doing that first one-and-a-half somersault was the greatest thrill of my life. I ran home and told my dad."

## Korean Pride

Sammy's father had come to America in 1905. He came from Korea, a country in Asia. The early 1900's was not a good time for Asian-Americans. At that time, many whites were **prejudiced**. They thought people of other races were not as good as whites.

prejudiced
thinking that certain groups of people are not as good as others

Sammy Lee had been born in America. But because he had Asian parents, he was often treated badly. Some places refused to let him in simply because he was Korean. Other places let him in, but made it clear that he wasn't really welcome.

Sammy's classmates liked him. They made him president of their high school class. Their parents, however, didn't always accept Sammy.

Mr. Lee had strong ideas about how Sammy could win the respect of white Americans. "First, you must always be proud of your Korean background," he said. "Also, you must get a good **education**. That will show people what kind of a person you are. And lastly, you should become a doctor. People need doctors. Sick people won't care about your race as long as you know how to make them well."

education
the training received at school

## The Diving Doctor

Sammy Lee agreed to his father's plan. He would try to become a doctor. He also wanted to keep diving. Sammy could get ready for **medical** school by studying hard. But how could he become a

medical
having to do with medicine

Sammy Lee practicing a reverse dive at the Olympics

better diver? Many pools in Los Angeles were closed to him.

Luckily, Sammy found a pool that was open to him. His skills grew with each practice. By 1938, he was one of the best divers in the city. But he needed a coach. He knew he would never make it to the Olympics without one. Most coaches were not interested in him. They didn't think an Asian could become a top athlete.

Then one day a man named Jim Ryan watched Sammy dive. Ryan had once been a great diver himself. He was now the best diving coach around. Ryan didn't care about the color of people's skin. He just wanted to coach the best young divers he could find. When he saw Sammy dive, he knew the boy had talent. He offered to become Sammy's coach.

With Ryan helping him, Sammy improved greatly. He was soon doing dives that no one else could do. He felt he was on his way to making the U.S. Olympic team.

At the same time, Sammy was studying to become a doctor. It wasn't easy. At first, he thought he might not make it. He almost **flunked** out of medical school. But he forced himself to study more, and he passed his courses.

In 1942, Sammy won his first U.S. diving **championship**. He then stopped diving for a short time to finish medical school. Sadly, his father didn't live to see him become a doctor. Mr. Lee died in 1943. In 1946, Sammy was back in the pool again. That year he won his second championship. Two years later in 1948, Sammy's dream came true. He won an Olympic gold medal in diving. He was the first full-blooded Asian to do so.

By 1952, Sammy had stopped diving. He was a doctor in the U.S. Army. Then the Olympic diving coach came to him. He asked Sammy to try out for that year's Olympic team. Sammy went to his commanding officer, General Leonard Heaton. "Sir, I would like to train for the Olympics. But I don't

**flunked**
kicked out of school because of failing grades

**championship**
contest to see who is the best

6

know if it's right for me to ask for time off while we're at war."

"Sam," said General Heaton, "we've got lots of doctors, but we've got only one guy who can win the Olympic medal in diving."

So once again, Sammy began training. In 1952 on his 32nd birthday, Sammy Lee won his second Olympic gold medal. He was the oldest diver ever to win a gold medal. He was also the first diver to win two gold medals in a row.

Sammy Lee celebrates with other medal winners.

# Vocabulary Skill Builder

■ Match each word with its meaning.

| | | | |
|---|---|---|---|
| ____ | 1. education | a. | people who play sports |
| ____ | 2. flunked | b. | had to leave school because of bad grades |
| ____ | 3. compete | c. | contest to see who is best |
| ____ | 4. athletes | d. | having to do with medicine |
| ____ | 5. championship | e. | rolling your body in a circle |
| ____ | 6. medical | f. | try to beat others |
| ____ | 7. somersault | g. | training received at school |

■ Write a paragraph using these three words from the story.

**prejudiced:**  thinking that certain groups of people are not as good as others

**talent:**  skill

**glory:**  honor and praise

_____

_____

_____

_____

_____

_____

_____

_____

# Read and Remember

■ Find the best ending for each sentence. Fill in the circle next to it.

1. Sammy Lee loved to
   ○ a. read.     ○ b. dive.     ○ c. go to parties.

2. Some people treated Sammy Lee badly because he was
   ○ a. young.     ○ b. a doctor.     ○ c. Asian-American.

3. Sammy's father wanted Sammy to
   ○ a. be a doctor.     ○ b. teach school.     ○ c. dive.

4. Jim Ryan offered to coach Sammy because
   ○ a. he liked him.     ○ b. he saw that Sammy had talent.
   ○ c. he felt sorry for Sammy.

5. Sammy Lee became the first diver to
   ○ a. do a somersault dive.     ○ b. win two gold medals in a row.
   ○ c. join the U.S. Army.

# Think and Apply—Finding the Sequence

■ Number the sentences to show the order in which things happened in the story. The first one is done for you.

____ Jim Ryan offered to be Sammy Lee's coach.

____ Sammy Lee won his second gold medal.

____ Sammy Lee became a doctor in the U.S. Army.

__1__ Sammy Lee did his first one-and-a-half somersault dive.

____ Sammy Lee won his first U.S. diving championship.

# Dawn Fraser

Swimming for
the Fun of It

**peak**
highest level

When Dawn Fraser was fourteen, she was spotted by a coach in a Sydney swimming pool.

He could see that she was a strong swimmer and hated to lose. "She was like a wild racehorse out of the hills," Coach Harry Gallagher said.

Dawn began training with Gallagher. At age fourteen, when many swimmers are reaching their **peak**, Dawn Fraser was just beginning to train.

## A Cheerful Attitude

By the time Dawn was eighteen, she had become a very strong swimmer. She won a spot on the 1956 Australian Olympic team. Each day she swam five to eight miles. Sometimes to make her arms stronger, she would pull an open oil drum behind her. She worked out in a gym. But Dawn also liked to have fun. If she didn't feel like swimming, she would take the day off and do something else.

Dawn Fraser with Canadian competitor at the 1956 Olympics

"I have a different **attitude** than most people," she said. "I **actually** enjoy training most of the time. When I don't want to train, I don't make myself."

**attitude**
way of thinking

**actually**
really

Dawn's attitude served her well. In the 1956 Olympics, she set a world record for the women's 100-meter **freestyle**. She also earned a gold medal. When the race was over, Dawn threw her arms around her parents. Tears of joy covered her face.

## Tragedy Strikes

Four years later, Dawn was back at the Olympics. She was 22 years old—old for a swimmer. Yet she remained **confident**. She felt she was still the world's best freestyle swimmer. Again Dawn walked away with a gold medal.

Dawn then looked ahead to the 1964 Olympics. No swimmer had ever won the same race three times. Dawn believed she could do it. In February of 1964, she felt as strong as ever. Then something **tragic** happened.

Dawn, her mother, and sister were driving home from a football game. They were in a terrible car accident. Dawn's mother was killed. Her sister was knocked out. Dawn herself was left with a chipped bone in her neck.

## An Amazing Recovery

For six weeks Dawn had a **cast** on her neck. It seemed that all dreams of a third gold medal were gone. She was 26 years old—old enough to be called "Granny" by other swimmers.

Her neck was in bad shape. And she was very sad about the loss of her mother.

Yet somehow Dawn began to bounce back. After her cast was removed, she returned to the pool. Seven months after the accident, she **shocked** everyone by winning another gold medal. She won the 100-meter race for the third straight time.

Dawn Fraser taking it easy after a practice swim

Dawn Fraser showed that she was the best woman swimmer in the world. When asked to explain her success, Dawn said, "I love water. It makes me feel **content** just to be in it. If I'm upset or in a **cranky** mood, I take a good long swim. I get fun out of swimming. It's as simple as that."

**content**
happy with the way things are

**cranky**
grouchy or unhappy

# Vocabulary Skill Builder

■ Complete the following sentences by writing the missing word in each space. Choose from the words in the box. When you are finished, the letters in the boxes will tell you what Olympic team Dawn Fraser was on.

| attitude | actually | cast | freestyle | confident |
|----------|----------|------|-----------|-----------|
| shocked | content | peak | cranky | tragic |

1. After her accident, Dawn's neck was in a _____ .

     __ ☐ __ __

2. Training was something that Dawn _____ enjoyed.

     __ __ __ ☐ __ __ __ __

3. When Dawn won her third gold medal, people were _____ .

     ☐ __ __ __ __ __ __

4. Swimming made Dawn feel _____ .

     __ __ __ ☐ __ __ __

5. Dawn took a long swim whenever she felt _____ .

     __ __ __ ☐ __ __

6. At fourteen, many swimmers reach their _____ .

     __ __ ☐ __

7. Dawn set a record in the 100-meter _____ .

     __ __ __ __ __ __ __ ☐ __

8. Dawn believed she had a good _____ .

     __ __ __ ☐ __ __ __ __

9. The loss of Dawn's mother was _____ .

     __ __ ☐ __ __ __

10. Even when others said she was too old to swim, Dawn remained _____ . __ __ __ __ __ __ __ ☐ __

# Read and Remember

■ Find the best ending for each sentence. Fill in the circle next to it.

1. Dawn became a swimmer because she
   ○ a. wanted to be famous.   ○ b. enjoyed swimming.   ○ c. was tall.

2. When Dawn didn't feel like swimming, she
   ○ a. took the day off.   ○ b. lifted weights.   ○ c. cried.

3. Dawn was called "Granny" because she was
   ○ a. old-fashioned.   ○ b. old for a swimmer.   ○ c. tired.

4. Dawn's mother was killed in a
   ○ a. car accident.   ○ b. plane crash.   ○ c. boating accident.

5. People were amazed when Dawn
   ○ a. married Harry Gallagher.   ○ b. became a singer.
   ○ c. won her third gold medal.

# Write Your Ideas

■ Pretend you are Dawn Fraser. You have been asked to give a short speech to young swimmers. Write what you would say.

_____

_____

_____

_____

_____

_____

_____

_____

_____

_____

# Jean-Claude Killy

## French Skiing Hero

The men and women who had come to Val d'Isère, France to ski just stood and watched. They couldn't believe their eyes. A young boy was zipping down the mountain at top speed.

"Look at him go," said one of the women. "Have you ever seen such a young boy go so fast?"

"Never," answered a man. "But that's Jean-Claude Killy. Even the best skiers around here have trouble keeping up with him."

## A Champion or a Disappointment?

The Killy family owned a ski **resort** in the French Alps. Jean-Claude got his first ski lesson in 1946, when he was three years old. By the time he was six, he could ski as fast as his father. He won his first race at age eight. At age ten, he could beat

**resort**
a place where people go on vacation

just about anyone in Val d'Isère. Later, as a world champion, he said, "I skied then almost as fast as I ski now, only I was always falling."

**future**
in the time yet to come

Killy skis the giant slalom.

At the age of seventeen, Jean-Claude was already on the French B team. The next year, he made the A team. Most people thought he was France's skiing star of the **future**. Killy copied the **styles** of the best skiers on the team. He **combined** these styles and came up with his own **successful** way of skiing.

**styles**
ways of doing something

**combined**
mixed together

**successful**
skillful

17

**disappointment**
a person who does not do as well as expected

But for several years, Jean-Claude was a **disappointment**. He had a string of bad luck. In 1962, he broke his leg. That finished him for the season. The next year he was ill. He kept skiing, but he did poorly.

French ski fans hoped Killy would shine in the 1964 Olympics. Jean-Claude was skiing in three races: the downhill, the **slalom**, and the giant slalom. The downhill is a high-speed race that takes great strength.

**slalom**
a race where skiers ski through gates

The slalom is a race through gates that are set close together. The giant slalom is a race through gates that are set farther apart. Jean-Claude didn't do well in any of these races. His sickness had left him weak. He fell in the downhill. He lost a ski in the slalom. And he finished fifth in the giant slalom.

Killy was not happy, but his luck was about to change. Starting in 1965, Jean-Claude won most of the races he entered. During the next two years, he led the French team to world championships. In both 1966-67 and 1967-68 he won the World Cup.

## Three Gold Medals

**goal**
something a person is working toward

Jean-Claude looked forward to the 1968 Olympics in Grenoble, France. His **goal** was to win all three races. This time he was ready. He was healthy and well-rested. He won the downhill by less than a tenth of a second. He won the giant slalom by over two seconds.

**rival**
someone racing against him

Things didn't go so smoothly in the slalom. Foggy weather made it hard to see the gates. Jean-Claude had a good run, but would he win the gold? He wouldn't know until he saw how his Austrian **rival**, Karl Schranz, did.

At first, **officials** said that Schranz had won the race. But two hours later, they changed the ruling. They said that Schranz had missed a gate.

**officials**
people in charge

Jean-Claude had won his third gold medal! He was only the second skier ever to do this. Ski fans across France cheered their hero. Jean-Claude Killy had finally proved how good he really was.

Killy at Olympic trials in Grenoble

# Vocabulary Skill Builder

■ Use the clues to complete the puzzle. Choose from the words in the box.

resort
future
styles
combined
successful
disappointment
slalom
goal
rival
officials

## Across

1. person who didn't do as well as expected
5. mixed together
6. another racer
7. what a person is working towards
8. ski race with gates
9. the time yet to come

## Down

2. skillful
3. people in charge
4. ways of doing something
6. place where people can go on vacation

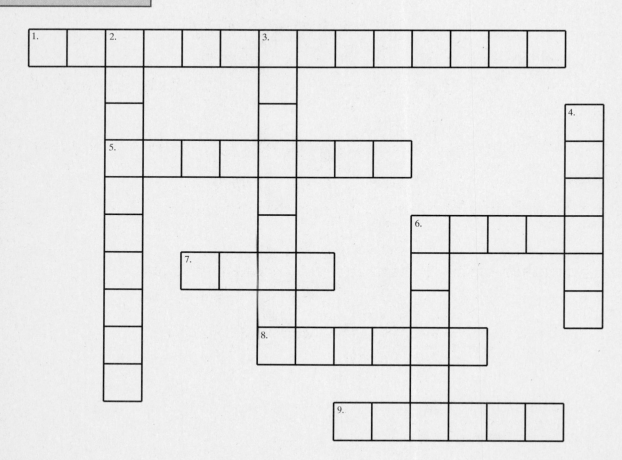

# Read and Remember

■ Some of the statements below are true. Others are false. Place a check in front of the three things that Jean-Claude Killy did.

_____ 1. Jean-Claude Killy got his first ski lesson at the age of three.

_____ 2. Jean-Claude Killy did poorly in his first Olympic Games.

_____ 3. Jean-Claude Killy raced against his father in the 1960 Olympics.

_____ 4. Jean-Claude Killy never learned how to ski the giant slalom.

_____ 5. Jean-Claude Killy broke his neck in a skiing accident.

_____ 6. Jean-Claude Killy beat Karl Schranz to win a third gold medal in the 1968 Olympics.

# Think and Apply—Drawing Conclusions

■ Finish each sentence by writing the best answer.

1. People in Val d'Isère thought young Jean-Claude Killy was a good skier because _____

2. Jean-Claude Killy studied the styles of the best skiers on his team because _____

3. Killy was unhappy after the 1964 Olympics because _____

_____

4. Foggy weather makes it hard for slalom racers because _____

_____

5. Killy became a French skiing hero because _____

_____

# Kip Keino

## Running His Own Race

**instructor**
teacher

**shrugged**
raised his shoulders
to show he didn't
know

"*L*ook at that guy run!" cried the head of the Police Training College. "Who is he, anyway?"

"That's Kip Keino," an **instructor** said. "He just started here. He's training to be a police officer."

"Where did he learn to run so fast?"

The instructor **shrugged**. "I don't know. He doesn't have any special training. I think he just taught himself."

## Born to Run

Kipchoge "Kip" Keino was born in a small village in the mountains of Kenya, a country in Africa. Kip ran track in high school. He set many school records. But he never took his running seriously. After high school, he returned to his father's farm to help care for the animals. After a year though, he grew tired of herding cattle.

In 1958, Kip entered the Police Training College in Kiganjo, Kenya. That was when people noticed what a good runner he really was. His instructors **suggested** he enter a few track races. By 1962, he was the best runner in all of Kenya.

**suggested**
put forward an idea

Keino wins 1500-meter race by more than 20 meters.

## A Runner Without a Coach

Unlike all the other top runners in the world, Kip did not have a coach. He trained by himself in the high mountains of Kenya. That was fine when he ran in **minor** races. But could he develop enough skills to win an Olympic gold medal?

**minor**
not important

Kip tried to do this in the 1964 Summer Olympics. He failed. He came in fifth in the 5,000 meter race. He didn't even get to run in the 1,500 meter race.

Even after his 1964 **defeat**, Kip still refused to get a coach. He wanted to become the world's best distance runner on his own. But he knew he needed more practice. "The only way I'll get better," he said to himself, "is to keep running against the top runners in the world."

For the next four years, he did just that. In 1965, he won six big races in Europe. He set a world record for 3,000 meters. He became the first African to run a mile in less than four minutes.

## Problems

Kip hoped to be in great shape for the 1968 Olympics. But early in 1968, he began to have stomach pains. Doctors told him to take it easy. They said that he shouldn't run in the Olympics. Kip **ignored** them. He entered the 10,000, 5,000, and 1,500 meter races—three long, hard races.

In the 10,000 meter race, Kip was running with the leaders with two laps to go. Suddenly, he **doubled** over in pain and fell to the ground. He got up and limped to the finish line far behind the winner. Four days later, he was back for the 5,000 meters. His stomach did not bother him that day. Still, the race was hard. He finished in second place.

"Be happy with your silver medal," a friend told him. "Don't run in the 1,500. Give your stomach a rest."

But Kip did not want to rest. He wanted to run,

**defeat**
loss

**ignored**
did not pay attention to

**doubled**
bent

24

and he wanted to win. On the day of the 1,500 meter race, he had one last problem. His **taxi** got caught in a traffic jam. He had to run a mile to the track. Even so, he breezed past the world's best runners that day. He won the 1,500 meter race by more than twenty meters. This was the largest **margin** of **victory** in that race in Olympic history!

**taxi**
car that takes a person somewhere

**margin**
amount of difference

**victory**
the winning of a contest

Keino at medal ceremony in Mexico City

# Vocabulary Skill Builder

## Part A

■ Match each word with its meaning.

____ 1. suggested      a. raised shoulders

____ 2. ignored      b. not important

____ 3. shrugged      c. put forward an idea

____ 4. instructor      d. did not pay attention to

____ 5. minor      e. teacher

## Part B

■ Read each sentence. Fill in the circle next to the best meaning for the word in dark print. If you need help, use the Glossary.

1. Keino did not give up after his 1964 **defeat.**
   ○ a. loss     ○ b. sickness     ○ c. fall

2. He stopped running and **doubled** over.
   ○ a. bent     ○ b. began moving backward     ○ c. walked

3. Keino's **taxi** got stuck in traffic.
   ○ a. parents     ○ b. coach     ○ c. a car paid to drive him

4. He won by a wide **margin.**
   ○ a. mistake     ○ b. amount     ○ c. change of rules

5. The **victory** made Keino very happy.
   ○ a. report     ○ b. speech     ○ c. winning of a contest

# Read and Remember

■ Answer the questions.

1. What did Kip Keino do when he got tired of herding cattle on his father's farm? _____

2. In what way was Kip Keino different from all the other top runners?

   _____

3. Why did doctors tell Keino not to run in the 1968 Olympics? _____

   _____

4. What happened to Keino during the 10,000 meter race? _____

   _____

5. What problem did Keino face on the day of the 1,500 meter race?

   _____

# Write Your Ideas

■ Pretend you are Kip Keino. Write a letter to a friend explaining why you want to train without a coach.

_____

_____

_____

_____

_____

_____

_____

_____

_____

_____

# Olga Korbut

## From Tears to Smiles

**nervous**
jumpy or afraid

**gymnasts**
people who jump
and tumble

**performance**
an act done in front
of judges

**competition**
contest

*S*eventeen-year-old Olga Korbut looked around her hotel room. She couldn't remember ever being this **nervous**.

"In a few hours, I will be performing in front of the whole world," she thought. "Now is my chance to make my dreams come true. But what if I fail?" She looked out the window. "What if I make a mistake?"

## No Room for Fear

Later that day, Olga Korbut walked into the Olympic gym. She smiled as she began warming up. She had pushed all thoughts out of her mind. Like all good **gymnasts**, she knew there was no room for fear during a **performance**.

At first, Olga did beautifully. It looked as though

she might win in the All-Around **competition**. This competition is made up of four events—balance beam, **vaulting**, **uneven parallel bars**, and floor exercises. As Olga got ready to get on the uneven parallel bars, she was excited. "I'm close," she thought. "If I do well here, I think I'll win the gold!"

**vaulting**
jumping over a padded box

**uneven parallel bars**
two bars, one set higher than the other

Olga Korbut performs a routine on the uneven parallel bars.

## Crushed Hopes

With a deep breath, Olga leaped on the bars. As she did so, her feet **scraped** along the floor. Her heart froze. She knew this mistake would lower her

**scraped**
rubbed against

Olga Korbut doing floor exercises at 1972 Olympics

score. The rest would have to be perfect. On one of her next moves, however, her hands slipped off the bars. She fell to the floor.

No one could believe it. Olga Korbut had fallen off the bars! This finished any chance she had of winning an All-Around medal. Olga stood up and tried to get back on the bars. Again she slipped. At last she got back up and finished her **routine**. But when it was over, she burst into tears.

**routine**
set of exercises done in a certain order

When people saw Olga weeping, their hearts went out to her. "Poor thing," people whispered, "she'll never get over this."

## Pulling It Together

Later that night, Olga sat silently in her hotel room. The All-Around competition was over. She had finished a poor seventh. But she could still win one of the four **individual** events. "I can't let my dream slip away," she thought. "I have to pull myself together and go back out there."

**individual**
single

That is exactly what she did. Less than 24 hours after her fall, Olga Korbut was back in front of the judges. As she began her floor exercises, her fans held their breath. They were all rooting for her. But people feared she had lost her confidence. They remembered her tears the night before.

This night, however, Olga seemed to shine with confidence. She wasn't thinking about mistakes. She was thinking only about what she was doing at that moment. A smile spread across her face as she danced and rolled and tumbled. Her moves were beautiful. And her joy seemed real. Her routine **dazzled** everyone. The crowd cheered wildly.

**dazzled**
amazed

By the end of the 1972 Olympics, Olga Korbut had won three gold medals—one for floor exercises, one for balance beam, and a third in team competition.

# Vocabulary Skill Builder

■ Write the best word to complete each sentence. Use each word once.

| performance | scraped | individual |
|---|---|---|
| nervous | uneven parallel bars | |

Olga Korbut was **(1)**_____ about being in the

Olympics. In one **(2)**_____ she had many problems.

She **(3)**_____ her feet on the floor. She also fell off

the **(4)**_____ . But Olga pulled herself together and

went on to win a gold medal with her team and gold medals in

two **(5)**_____ events.

## Part B

■ Match each word with its meaning.

____ 1. gymnasts     a. jumping over a padded box

____ 2. dazzled     b. amazed

____ 3. vaulting     c. contest

____ 4. routine     d. people who jump and tumble

____ 5. competition     e. set of exercises done in a certain order

# Read and Remember

■ Some of the statements below are true. Others are false. Place a check in front of the three things that Olga Korbut did.

_____ 1. Olga Korbut won the gold medal for the All-Around competition.

_____ 2. Olga Korbut broke her leg while vaulting.

_____ 3. Olga Korbut fell off the balance beam.

_____ 4. Olga Korbut cried after she finished her routine on the uneven parallel bars.

_____ 5. Olga Korbut dazzled people with her floor exercise routine.

_____ 6. Olga Korbut won three gold medals.

# Think and Apply—Main Ideas

■ Underline the two most important ideas from the story.

1. Olga Korbut was usually able to keep fear out of her mind during performances.

2. People felt sorry for Olga Korbut when they saw her crying.

3. After one poor performance, Olga Korbut came back to win three gold medals.

4. Olga Korbut stayed in a hotel during the 1972 Olympics.

5. Olga Korbut was just seventeen years old when she competed in the 1972 Olympic Games.

# Greg Louganis

## Facing His Fears

**platform**
a flat surface raised
up off the ground

Greg Louganis stood on the diving **platform**. He looked down at the water 33 feet below. Then he looked away. He wanted to try the new dive, but he was afraid. After several minutes, Greg climbed down off the platform.

"What's wrong?" asked coach Ron O'Brien.

"I can't do it," said Greg softly.

"Look," O'Brien said. "Even if you have to eat dinner off the platform tomorrow, you're going to stay there until you learn that dive!"

## A Dangerous Dive

Ron O'Brien was helping Greg Louganis get ready for the 1984 U.S. Olympic team. "You're a great diver," O'Brien told Greg. "But to win a gold medal, you have to do more difficult dives."

O'Brien wanted Greg to learn a **reverse** 3 1/2 somersault. Only a few people had ever done this dive. The dive brings the diver's head dangerously close to the platform. Most divers refused to try it.

Greg looked at O'Brien. Then he nodded. "You're right," he said. "If I want to be the best in the world, I have to do this dive."

Fighting to block out his fear, Greg climbed back onto the platform. He took a deep breath. Then he began the dive. As he hit the water, he smiled. He had done it!

**reverse**
backward

Louganis performing a reverse dive

Greg practiced his reverse 3 1/2 somersault many times as he prepared for the 1984 Olympics. Each time it got a little easier for him. Still, it remained **risky**. In 1983, a top Russian diver tried the same dive. The Russian hit his head on the platform. He fell into the water, badly hurt. He died one week later. Greg Louganis kept practicing the dive. But he tried to be more careful than ever.

## The Making of a Great Diver

Greg Louganis had started diving as a young boy. It was not a happy time for him. He was having trouble in school. He saw words backwards. When

**risky**
dangerous

Louganis dives off the springboard.

he looked at the word "bird" he saw "drib." This made it very hard for him to read. Other kids laughed at him. They teased him because he was a poor reader. They also made fun of his dark skin. Greg was **adopted** shortly after he was born in 1960. His skin color came from his birth father. He was from Samoa in the South Pacific.

Without many friends, Greg turned to diving. He liked the sport because he could do it alone. He quickly became very good. At the age of eleven, he scored a perfect ten at the Junior Olympics. One coach said, "His spring off the board was so much higher than that of anyone else. Greg was years ahead of his age group."

At sixteen, Greg made it to the 1976 Olympics. He was so excited that he had trouble thinking about his dives. He finished sixth in **springboard** diving and second in platform diving. This disappointed him. He had hoped to win a gold.

Greg could not go to the 1980 Olympics. The United States did not send a team that year. So he and his coach began working toward 1984. When those Olympics arrived, Greg was ready. In the springboard contest, he amazed everyone with his dives. He won the gold medal easily.

Next came platform diving. This was where Greg planned to do his reverse 3 1/2 somersault. If he did it well, he would win a second gold medal. But Greg was nervous. One mistake would cost him the gold.

Quietly Greg stepped up to the platform. He leaped into the air and **tucked** his body. The dive was beautiful. It won him a second gold medal!

**adopted**
brought into someone's family and raised as his or her own child

**springboard**
a board that bounces divers high into the air

**tucked**
curled into a ball

# One More Push for the Gold

After the 1984 Olympics, some people thought Louganis would give up diving. But Greg wanted to try for two more gold medals.

When the 1988 Olympics opened, Greg Louganis was there. But he was not feeling well. He had a **fever** and a sore throat. His wrist hurt. The other divers all looked so young and fresh. The best was China's Xiong Ni. Xiong was only fourteen—half as old as Greg.

"Maybe this was a mistake," Greg thought to himself. "Maybe I should have quit while I was ahead." But it was too late to quit. He was part of the U.S. team. He would have to do his best.

Greg got off to a terrible start in the **trial** dives. On his ninth dive, he jumped too close to the springboard. As he spun through the air, he cracked his head on the board. Greg fell into the water. When he climbed out, doctors rushed over. They put five stitches in the top of his head.

Coach Ron O'Brien knew Greg had to do two more dives right away. If he didn't, he would be dropped from the competition. O'Brien took Greg aside. He said, "Look, **hockey** players get 50 stitches and then go back on the ice. You can do two more dives."

Greg smiled. "Okay," he said, "I'll try."

Slowly he climbed back up to the board. He did his next two dives without mistakes.

The next morning, the finals were held. Greg dived beautifully. For his last dive, he did his reverse 3 1/2 somersault. That earned him the gold medal.

**fever**
when a person's body is hotter than it should be

**trial**
test to see who can be in the final competition

**hockey**
a game that skaters play on ice

Louganis dives in 1984 Olympics.

"Now," thought Greg, "if I can only do as well in the platform diving."

On the platform, Chinese diver Xiong Ni looked strong. His dives were nearly perfect. Greg needed a great dive to win the gold. To stay **calm**, he whispered these words: "No matter what happens, my mother will still love me."

Then he jumped. His dive was the reverse 3 1/2 somersault. He did it better than ever before. When the scores were posted, Greg Louganis broke into tears. He had his fourth gold medal! He had beaten Xiong Ni by just one point—638 to 637.

**calm**
not excited or upset

# Vocabulary Skill Builder

■ Use the clues to complete the puzzle. Choose from the words in the box.

platform
reverse
risky
adopted
springboard
tucked
fever
trial
hockey
calm

## Across

2. test
4. a raised surface
6. backward
8. a board that divers bounce on
9. curled into a ball

## Down

1. not worried
3. brought into a family and raised as part of that family
5. when a person's body is too hot
6. dangerous
7. a game skaters play on ice

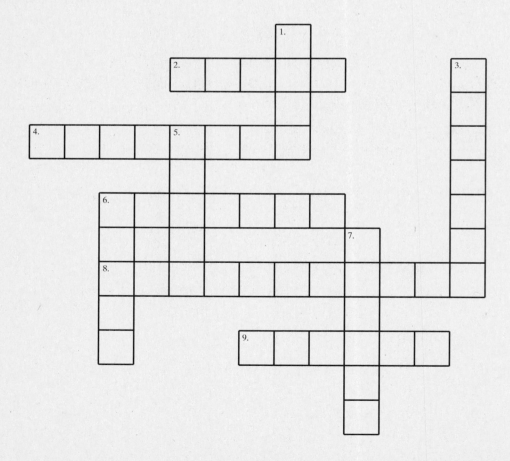

# Read and Remember

■ Answer the questions.

1. Why is the reverse 3 1/2 somersault such a dangerous dive? _____

    _____

2. What happened when Greg Louganis was eleven? _____

    _____

3. How did Greg Louganis do at the 1984 Olympics? _____

    _____

4. What did Ron O'Brien tell Greg to do after Greg hit his head on
    the springboard? _____

5. What did Greg say to himself to stay calm as he tried to win his
    fourth gold medal? _____

    _____

# Write Your Ideas

■ Pretend you are Greg Louganis. Give a speech to a group of
children. Tell about the problems you had during your childhood
and how diving helped you.

_____

_____

_____

_____

_____

_____

_____

_____

# Scott
# Hamilton
## Standing Tall

**syndrome**
a set of problems
with a person's body

"**M**r. and Mrs. Hamilton," said the doctor, "we think we found out what's wrong with your son."

Ernie Hamilton held his wife's hand. "What is it? Why has Scotty stopped growing?"

"Scott has Schwachmann's **syndrome**," answered the doctor. "It's a stomach problem. Scotty's stomach doesn't work the way it should. That means his body isn't getting the food it needs to grow."

## Searching for the Truth

Scott Hamilton was born in 1958. He seemed to be a happy, healthy little boy. Then, at the age of two, something strange happened. He suddenly stopped growing.

His parents took him to the hospital. The doctors

**suspected** he had a stomach problem. But they didn't know for sure what it was or how to treat it. They started guessing. "One doctor put him on a special no-milk **diet** for a year," Ernie Hamilton later said. "But all that did was to starve the poor little kid."

The Hamiltons grew more and more worried. Their son still wasn't growing. They took Scott to see other doctors. He was sent to one hospital after another. Every doctor had a different idea. One thought Scotty was dying. This doctor told the Hamiltons their son had only six months to live.

**suspected**
thought something might be true

**diet**
the food that someone eats

Hamilton performs his long program in 1984 Olympics.

Finally, when Scott was eight years old, the Hamiltons took him to Boston Children's Hospital in Massachusetts. There, doctors discovered the truth. They put a special feeding tube into his stomach. They also told him to get some exercise. "We aren't sure," one of the doctors said, "but we think exercise might help people with Schwachmann's syndrome. It certainly won't hurt."

## Problems Disappear

The doctors told the Hamiltons there wasn't much else they could do. With the feeding tube in place, Scott would start growing again. But he had lost six years of **growth**. He would never be as big as other people.

**growth**
getting taller

Mr. and Mrs. Hamilton took Scott back home to Bowling Green, Ohio. Soon after that, they took him to a skating **rink**. His older sister Susan wanted to go ice skating. The Hamiltons thought Scott might like to watch.

**rink**
an area covered with ice for skating

Scott sat in the cold rink. He watched Susan glide across the ice. Suddenly he turned to his father. He said, "You know, I think I'd like to try skating."

As soon as Scott stepped out onto the ice, he loved the sport. He discovered that he could skate with speed and **grace**. Every day he got better and better. In a few months, he even joined his school's ice hockey team. As he later said, "I had finally found something I could do as well as everyone else."

**grace**
moving the body in a smooth, beautiful way

Something else was happening, as well. After a year of skating, Scott went back to see his doctor. The doctor couldn't believe his eyes. "What have you done to this boy?" he asked Mr. Hamilton. "He's healthy!"

What happened to Scott was something of a **miracle**. His stomach problems had disappeared. The doctors decided the change was caused by the cool, damp air of the ice rink and all that exercise. Scott later said, "I just skated my way out of it."

**miracle**
something wonderful that cannot be explained

## Larger Than Life

In 1971, at the age of thirteen, Scott began to compete against the best young skaters in the country. By 1979, he believed he could make the Olympic team. But one day a skating judge took

Hamilton waits with his coaches to learn his score.

Hamilton celebrates his gold medal on the ice.

him aside. "Let me tell you something," the judge said. "Don't get your hopes up. You'll never be a world champion."

"Why not?" asked Scott angrily.

"You're too small," said the judge. "The judges just won't take you seriously."

Scott didn't know what to say. He went home and thought about what the judge had said. He didn't want to give up the sport he loved. But there was nothing he could do about his size. He was 5 feet, 3 inches tall and weighed 110 pounds. "Perhaps I AM too short to be a world-class skater," he said to himself. But then he had another thought. "Maybe, just maybe, I can find a way to look taller than I really am."

The next day Scott went out on the ice and began to experiment. He tried new kinds of jumps. He tried different **takeoffs** and landings. On every move, he stretched out his body to **create** longer lines.

**takeoffs**
leaving the ice to jump in the air

**create**
make

"It's working!" his coach said after several weeks. "This new style really does make you look taller."

In 1980, Scott Hamilton made the United States winter Olympic team. He skated well and finished in fifth place. Scott was happy. He had proved that he could skate with the top men in the world. "You see?" he told his friends. "Skaters don't have to be tall. They only have to seem tall."

Scott wasn't ready to give up skating. So for the next three years, he kept going. He practiced eight hours a day, six days a week. He entered fifteen skating competitions and won them all.

In 1984, he returned to the Olympics. There the tiny kid from Bowling Green showed the world what he could do. He showed off his strong jumps and quick turns. In doing so, he **captured** a gold medal. On the night he won, he said, "I did it. I really wanted this night to be something special, and it was."

**captured**
won

# Vocabulary Skill Builder

■ Complete the following sentences by writing the missing word in each space. Choose from the words in the box. When you are finished, the letters in the boxes will describe Scott Hamilton as a young boy.

| miracle | suspected | diet | takeoffs | captured |
|---------|-----------|------|----------|----------|
| growth  | create    | rink | syndrome | grace    |

1. Scott was proud of the gold medal he _____ .

   __ ☐ __ __ __ __ __ __ __

2. Stomach problems caused Scott to stop growing, the doctors _____ .

   __ __ ☐ __ __ __ __ __ __ __

3. One doctor put Scott on a no-milk _____ .

   __ ☐ __ __

4. Scott learned to skate with speed and _____ .

   __ __ __ ☐ __

5. Scott learned to stretch his body during _____ .

   __ __ ☐ __ __ __ __ __

6. Long body lines were what Scott tried to _____ .

   ☐ __ __ __ __ __ __

7. Scott lost six years of _____ .

   __ __ __ __ __ __ ☐

8. Scott watched his sister skating around the _____ .

   __ ☐ __ __

9. What happened to Scott was a kind of _____ .

   __ __ __ __ __ __ ☐ __

10. Scott had Schwachmann's _____ .

    __ __ __ ☐ __ __ __

for 8th
graders
wed

4 5 8 9 10 11 12 15 16 17 18 19 22 23 24 25 26 27 30 1 2 3

# Read and Remember

■ Some of the statements below are true. Others are false. Place a check in front of the three things that happened in the story.

____  1. Ice skating caused Scott Hamilton to become very sick.

____  2. Scott Hamilton stopped growing for six years.

____  3. A judge told Scott Hamilton he was too short to be a world champion skater.

____  4. Scott's sister, Susan, won a gold medal in the 1984 Olympics.

____  5. Scott learned to make himself look taller on the ice than he really was.

____  6. Scott Hamilton died in Ohio in 1984.

# Think and Apply—Cause and Effect

■ Complete the following sentences.

1. Mr. and Mrs. Hamilton took Scott to many doctors because _____

_____

2. A doctor told Scott to exercise because _____

_____

_____

3. The Hamiltons took Scott to a skating rink for the first time because

_____

4. Scott would never be as big as other people because _____

_____

5. Scott experimented with new kinds of jumps because _____

_____

# Kristi Yamaguchi

## Winning With Style

**twirled**
spun

*F*our-year-old Kristi Yamaguchi moved closer to the TV set. She wanted to get a better look at the Olympic skaters on the screen. Kristi watched in wonder as the women danced, jumped, and **twirled** around the ice.

Kristi turned to her parents. She said, "That's what I want to do when I grow up."

"We'll see, Kristi," laughed her father. "You're still pretty little. Maybe you can try skating in a year or two."

## Hard Work
Kristi finally got on the ice when she was six years old. Her parents agreed to let her take skating lessons. By the age of eight, she was skating in competitions. She still dreamed of making it to the

Olympics. But many other girls shared that dream. If she was going to rise to the top, she would have to work very hard.

Kristi began spending hours each day on the ice. Every morning she got up at four o'clock. She practiced for several hours before going to school. "It wasn't so bad," she later said. "I got used to it. Besides, the skating made it **worthwhile**."

**worthwhile**
worth all the time and work put into something

Kristi Yamaguchi during a competition

51

In 1983, at the age of twelve, Kristi found a skating partner. His name was Rudi Galindo. Kristi and Rudi entered competitions as pairs skaters. Kristi also kept working as a singles skater. In 1988, she was the junior world champion in both events. A year later, she and Rudi finished fifth in the world **senior** pairs competition. Kristi finished sixth in the singles.

**senior**
skaters who are at least eighteen years old

Kristi Yamaguchi during her long program

Most top skaters do not do both kinds of skating. It is too **demanding**. They choose one or the other. Then they put all their work in that direction. Kristi, however, didn't want to choose. She liked both kinds of skating. And she was willing to work hard on each one. As her singles coach said, "I don't think she ever thinks of being tired."

By 1990, though, Kristi had to choose. She was doing her pairs training at home in California. But her singles coach had moved to Canada. Kristi was flying between the two places to train. She knew she couldn't do that forever. After a lot of thought, she went to see Rudi.

"I have to choose between singles and pairs," she told him. "You and I are good together, but we're not the best. I think we've gone as far as we can together. So from now on, I'm only going to do singles."

## On Her Own

It was hard for Kristi to say good-by to Rudi. But once she did, her singles skating got better. She no longer had to split her time between two places and two kinds of skating. She could spend all her time on her singles **program**. Soon she was beating the best singles skaters in the world.

Kristi knew her success might not last. The world of figure skating is tough. Few skaters stay on top for long. As Kristi said in 1989, "Anything can happen. There are always new skaters coming up."

Perhaps the biggest problem for Kristi was the "**triple** axel." It is the most difficult jump in ice skating. The skater has to make three and a half turns in the air before landing. The first woman to

**demanding**
calling for a great deal of time and hard work

**program**
an act made up of certain moves and skills

**triple**
three of something

do a triple axel was Midori Ito of Japan. Midori won the 1989 world competition by doing the jump. In 1991, Kristi hoped to win the National Championships. But this time Tonya Harding beat her by landing a perfect triple axel.

Kristi could do all the other triple jumps. And she could do them faster and better than anyone else. But she hadn't **mastered** the triple axel. Did that mean she would never beat women like Midori and Tonya?

## A Dream Comes True

In 1992, Kristi's dream came true. She won a spot on the U.S. Olympic team. People thought she would do well. But they wondered if she could win the gold without the triple axel. News **reporters** kept asking her about it.

Kristi, however, believed there was more to skating than just one jump. "Skating is an **art**," she said. "I still have seven triples in my program. Maybe that's not up to the triple axel that Midori and Tonya have, but it is one of the most difficult programs."

Finally the 1992 Olympics arrived. Thousands of people came to watch the skating. Millions more watched on TV. Kristi was nervous as she got ready to skate. The other women were nervous, too. Each one was hoping to win the gold medal.

Midori Ito looked great as she began her program. But as she went for the triple axel, she **stumbled**. The same thing happened to Tonya Harding. Kristi Yamaguchi had no triple axel to worry about. In the words of one writer, Kristi skated "as if all that mattered was making people smile."

**mastered**
learned to do well

**reporters**
people who write for newspapers and magazines

**art**
something that has beauty and special meaning

**stumbled**
lost her balance

Kristi Yamaguchi won the highest score from all nine judges. That gave her the gold medal! Reporters crowded around her. They all wanted to know what she was thinking. "I've dreamed about this since I was a little girl and I first put on a pair of skates," she said. "To think about how far I've come, it's all still sinking in." With that, Kristi smiled and skated off to collect her gold medal.

Kristi Yamaguchi prepares for a spin.

# Vocabulary Skill Builder

## Part A

■ Match each word with its meaning.

____ 1. art

____ 2. reporters

____ 3. twirled

____ 4. seniors

____ 5. triple

____ 6. stumbled

____ 7. program

a. three of something

b. spun around

c. lost one's balance

d. skaters who are at least eighteen years old

e. an act made up of certain moves and skills

f. people who write for newspapers and magazines

g. something that has beauty and special meaning

## Part B

■ Write a paragraph using these three words from the story.

**worthwhile:** worth all the time and work
**mastered:** learned to do well
**demanding:** calling for a great deal of time and hard work

_____

_____

_____

_____

_____

_____

_____

_____

# Read and Remember

■ Find the best ending for each sentence. Fill in the circle next to it.

1. Kristi was willing to work hard at skating because she
   ○ a. needed the money.    ○ b. wanted to make her parents happy.
   ○ c. hoped to make it to the Olympics.

2. Kristi told Rudi she was going to stop
   ○ a. singles skating.    ○ b. pairs skating.
   ○ c. both singles and pairs skating.

3. At the age of twelve, Kristi
   ○ a. found a skating partner.    ○ b. moved to Canada.
   ○ c. was in a terrible accident.

4. The first woman to do a triple axel was
   ○ a. Kristi Yamaguchi.    ○ b. Tonya Harding.    ○ c. Midori Ito.

5. Kristi won the gold medal without doing
   ○ a. any jumps.    ○ b. a triple axel.    ○ c. any practicing.

# Write Your Ideas

Write three important facts you learned from this story.

1. _____

_____

_____

2. _____

_____

_____

3. _____

_____

_____

# Jackie Joyner-Kersee

## The Best Ever

$J$ackie Joyner was born on March 3, 1962. When her grandmother came to see her in the hospital, she studied the baby for a long moment. "You should name this baby after President Kennedy's wife—Jacqueline," she told Mary and Alfred Joyner. "One day this girl will be the first lady of something," she **predicted**.

## A Bad Neighborhood

Jackie Joyner grew up in East St. Louis, Illinois. Her family lived in one of the worst neighborhoods in the city. It was dangerous just to be out on the streets. **Crime** and **violence** were everywhere.

Many times Jackie and her older brother Al would listen to glass breaking and men shouting out in the street. In 1973, when Jackie was just eleven

**predicted**
made a guess about what would happen

**Crime**
acts that are against the law

**violence**
using force to cause harm

years old, she saw a man shot and killed outside her house.

Jackie's family had little money. Their house had thin walls and tiny rooms. Every winter the water pipes froze. They had to heat water on the stove to take baths.

Jackie throws the javelin in the 1988 Olympics.

Sometimes Jackie felt she would never escape from this neighborhood. Her parents, however, were strong people. They had high hopes for their children. Mrs. Joyner made sure Jackie worked

Jackie jumping hurdles in the 1988 Olympics

hard in school and stayed out of trouble. By the time Jackie was eleven, she believed she COULD make a better life for herself. One way to do that was through school. The other way was through sports.

Jackie loved sports. She was a **volleyball** star at her school. She was also a leader on the basketball team. But it was in track and field that Jackie really shined. In 1979, she set a new state high school record for the long jump. The next year she beat her own record by two inches.

After Jackie took up track and field, her brother Al decided to try it, too. He turned out to be a great jumper. But Al didn't always feel like practicing. That was when Jackie would step in. She pushed him to keep training. She even dragged him out of bed some mornings so he would get to practice.

## Gold for Al, Silver for Jackie

In 1981, Jackie won a **scholarship** to UCLA. She began playing college basketball. She also worked on her long jump. One day UCLA coach Bob Kersee called her aside. Kersee could see that Jackie was a great athlete. "You should be doing more track and field," he told her. "Have you ever thought about the heptathlon?"

The heptathlon is the hardest track and field event a woman can do. It is made up of seven parts. These are: the 100-meter **hurdles**, the shot put, the high jump, the 200-meter run, the long jump, the **javelin**, and the 800-meter run. An athlete might be good at one part. But few people can do all seven parts well.

At first, Jackie wasn't interested. She wanted to stick with basketball and the long jump. Kersee talked her out of that. He told her she could win a gold medal in the heptathlon. By 1983, Jackie agreed. She spent all her time working on the heptathlon.

**volleyball**
a game where players use their hands to hit a ball back and forth across a net

**scholarship**
money given to a student to pay for school

**hurdles**
a series of bars that runners jump over

**javelin**
a spear that is thrown

61

**injury**
damage done to the body

At the 1984 Olympics, Jackie had a chance for the gold medal. But a leg **injury** was slowing her down. As she began the 800-meter race, she seemed to have lost her strength. It looked as though she would finish far behind the winner.

Al Joyner was watching from the side lines. He, too, was competing at these Olympics. Like his sister, he had become a track and field star. Al's sport was the triple jump. But as he watched Jackie run, he forgot about himself.

**infield**
the area inside a track

"This is Jackie's big chance," he thought. "I can't let her give up without a fight." Quickly Al ran across the **infield** of the track. He ran along the inside of the track, shouting to Jackie. "Pump your arms, Jackie!" he yelled. "This is it!"

Jackie competes in the long jump in Barcelona.

When Jackie heard Al's voice, she found new strength. She began running faster. She finished the race less than two seconds behind the winner.

Jackie did not win the gold medal that year. She won the silver. Al had come away with a gold medal in the triple jump. When Jackie saw Al, she was so happy for him that she burst into tears.

But Jackie also wanted to win a gold medal of her own. In her heart, she knew she could do it. So she went back to California to continue her training.

## An All-Around Special Person

Over the next two years, Jackie fell in love with Bob Kersee. They were married in 1986. Kersee continued to coach her. With his help, Jackie became even stronger. By 1988, she had the best heptathlon scores in the world.

At the 1988 Olympics, Jackie breezed through the seven parts of the heptathlon. Her final score was far above everyone else's. Four years later, she returned to win her second Olympic heptathlon. By then, people were calling her the world's greatest woman athlete. Jackie, however, knew that her greatest victory did not come at the Olympics. It came in escaping the crime and **poverty** of her early years.

**poverty**
having little or no money

"I remember where I came from," she said. "And I keep that in mind." To help the children in her old neighborhood, Jackie rented a plane. She took 114 kids from East St. Louis to New York City to see the 1991 Thanksgiving Day parade. "People think it's special to be an all-around athlete," she said. "But it's more important to be an all-around person."

# Vocabulary Skill Builder

■ Write the best word to complete each sentence. Use each word once.

| | | | | |
|---|---|---|---|---|
| javelin | predicted | volleyball | crime | scholarship |

Jackie Joyner-Kersee grew up in a neighborhood with

much (1)_____ . In high school she was a star

(2)_____ player. After high school, she was given a

(3)_____ to UCLA. There she began to try new sports

such as the high jump and the (4)_____ . As her

grandmother had (5)_____ , Jackie Joyner-Kersee became

the "first lady" of the Olympic heptathlon.

■ Read each sentence. Fill in the circle next to the best meaning for the word in dark print. If you need help, use the Glossary.

1. In East St. Louis, Illinois, **violence** seemed to be everywhere.
   ○ a. purple flowers    ○ b. the use of force    ○ c. high fences

2. The 100-meter **hurdles** is part of the heptathlon.
   ○ a. animals    ○ b. tall buildings
   ○ c. races where runners jump over bars

3. A leg **injury** slowed Jackie down in the 1984 Olympics.
   ○ a. damage to the body    ○ b. bandage    ○ c. very tight clothes

4. Jackie's brother Al quickly crossed the **infield.**
   ○ a. line on the ground    ○ b. inside of the track    ○ c. long jump

5. Jackie Joyner-Kersee found a way to escape **poverty.**
   ○ a. having no money   ○ b. a prison room   ○ c. people with guns

## Read and Remember
■ Answer the questions.

1. What was the Joyner family house like? _____

_____

2. Why did Jackie sometimes drag her brother Al out of bed? _____

_____

3. What did Bob Kersee tell Jackie after he saw her training at UCLA?

_____

4. What did Jackie do when she heard Al shouting to her in the
   800-meter race of the 1984 Olympics? _____

_____

5. What did Jackie Joyner-Kersee think was her greatest victory? _____

_____

## Think and Apply—Fact or Opinion?
■ Write **F** before each fact. Write **O** before each opinion.

_____ 1. Mr. and Mrs. Joyner had high hopes for their children.

_____ 2. The Joyner family should have moved out of East St. Louis.

_____ 3. The long jump is the easiest part of the heptathlon.

_____ 4. Al Joyner tried to help Jackie win a gold medal in 1984.

_____ 5. Jackie Joyner played basketball at UCLA.

_____ 6. Students at UCLA spend too much time playing sports.

_____ 7. Bob Kersee is the best coach ever.

# Pablo Morales

## The Comeback of a Lifetime

*P*ablo Morales stepped up on the starting block. He swung his arms in wide, slow circles. Seven other swimmers did the same thing. They were getting ready to swim the 100-meter butterfly in the 1984 Olympics. At last the starter called out, "Take your mark!"

A moment later the race began. Pablo quickly took the lead. As he touched the finish wall, he thought to himself, "I've won!" Then he looked up at the **scoreboard**. His heart sank. Pablo had finished second.

## More Disappointments

Pablo Morales had **expected** to win the 100-meter butterfly. Going into the 1984 Olympics, he held the world record in this event. Pablo did swim well in the race. But West Germany's Michael Gross swam even better. In the last few meters Gross passed Pablo. That gave Gross a new world record and a gold medal.

Pablo Morales swimming 100-meter butterfly

Pablo was disappointed. Still, he **vowed** to keep swimming. He began training for a gold medal in 1988. In 1986, he beat Michael Gross's time. Once again Pablo held the world record. By the 1988 Olympics, he was a huge **favorite** to win the 100-meter butterfly. He also hoped to win gold medals in two other events.

**vowed**
promised

**favorite**
the person who is believed to have the best chance of winning

Then came the big shock. Pablo Morales never got to the 1988 Olympics. He swam poorly in the trial races. He failed to make the United States team in any of the three events. "All I did was train like a horse," Pablo said. "When it came time to race, I didn't have anything left."

## One Last Try

failure
loss

After this **failure**, Pablo wanted nothing to do with swimming. He had tried his best, and he had lost. "Now," he thought, "I've got to get on with my life." That fall he started law school. For three years, he stayed out of the water.

Then, in 1991, Pablo began to wonder. "Could I still swim with the world's best? Should I give it one more try?" Pablo was no longer in top shape. His **muscles** had grown soft. And at the age of 27, he was much older than most other Olympic swimmers. Still, he decided to try a **comeback**. "I don't know what to expect," Pablo said. "I just want to see."

muscles
the parts of the body that give a person strength

comeback
to leave a sport, then return to it and become good again

amazement
surprise

Pablo swam in one race before the 1992 Olympic trials. He lost. After that, he didn't bother to race. He just stuck to training and hoped it would be enough. To everyone's **amazement**, he did well in the trials. He made the Olympic team in the 100-meter butterfly.

## The Glory of the Gold

This time, no one expected Pablo to win a gold medal. But that didn't matter. Pablo was where he wanted to be. "All I want is a chance," he said. "I want a chance for glory and a chance to prove myself against the best."

Pablo had a simple race plan. He hoped to grab a

quick lead and hold it. He knew the other swimmers would close on him at the end. That is exactly what happened. As he neared the finish wall, the others were catching up to him.

Then the race was over. For several moments, Pablo was afraid to look at the scoreboard. He remembered all too well what had happened in 1984. At last he looked up. He saw his name in first place. He had won!

After the race Pablo tried to **express** his joy. He said, "In life we don't always **realize** our goals. And not all of our dreams come true. But this one did!"

**express**
put into words

**realize**
reach

Morales after seeing his winning time

# Vocabulary Skill Builder

■ Use the clues to complete the puzzle. Choose from the words in the box.

| scoreboard |
| expected |
| vowed |
| favorite |
| failure |
| muscles |
| comeback |
| amazement |
| express |
| realize |

## Across

2. to return to a sport and become good again
6. promised
7. reach
9. put into words
10. loss

## Down

1. the person believed to have the best chance of winning
3. parts of the body that make you strong
4. complete surprise
5. sign that shows scores
8. thought likely to happen

70

## Read and Remember

■ Find the best ending for each sentence. Fill in the circle next to it.

1. In 1984, Pablo Morales was disappointed because he did not
   ○ a. win a gold medal.   ○ b. do well in school.   ○ c. make money.

2. People were shocked in 1988 when Pablo did not
   ○ a. return from Puerto Rico.   ○ b. make the Olympic team.
   ○ c. shake Michael Gross's hand.

3. For three years Pablo did not
   ○ a. speak to his father.   ○ b. eat meat.   ○ c. swim.

4. While in law school, Pablo began to wonder if he could still
   ○ a. swim with the world's best.   ○ b. run fast.
   ○ c. wear his gold medal.

5. In 1992, no one expected Pablo Morales to
   ○ a. watch TV.   ○ b. win a gold medal.   ○ c. become a lawyer.

## Write Your Ideas

■ Pretend you are a newspaper reporter. Write three questions that you would want to ask Pablo Morales after he won his gold medal.

1. _____

_____

_____

2. _____

_____

_____

3. _____

_____

_____

# Gail Devers

## Dash for Glory

Gail Devers sat in the office of her coach, Bob Kersee. Her whole body was shaking. "I don't know what's wrong with me," she said. "My hair is falling out. My head hurts all the time. And I've lost ten pounds in the last month."

Kersee put his arm around Gail's shoulder. "Go see the doctor," he said. "Find out what's wrong. When you get your health back, you'll be running around the track faster than ever."

## What's Wrong With Me?

Gail Devers did go to a doctor. He told her she had been training too hard. He said her body was just tired and run down.

That seemed to make sense. Gail HAD been working hard. She was on the U.S. track and field team. She had just come back from the 1988 Olympics.

"Maybe that's why I ran so poorly at the Olympics," Gail thought. "I guess my body needs a rest."

Gail Devers coming out of the blocks during 100-meter heat

Gail cut back her training. Still, her health got worse. She lost the sight in her left eye. She had trouble remembering things. She couldn't sleep at night. She went to other doctors, but they had no answers. By early 1989, Gail was too sick to run at all. Months passed. Finally, in 1990, doctors found out what was wrong.

**thyroid**
the part of the body that controls how fast food is burned

**energy**
the power to do work

**radiation**
a powerful kind of wave that travels through the air

**Blisters**
sore spots on the skin that look like little bubbles

**swollen**
puffed up beyond something's usual size

**amputated**
cut off

**heal**
get better

"Your **thyroid** isn't working right," they said. The thyroid is the part of the body that controls how fast the body burns **energy**. Because Gail's thyroid was not working right, her whole body was out of control.

Doctors began giving Gail **radiation** treatment. "You'll feel better soon," they promised. The radiation did help. Gail's health problems faded away. In February of 1991, she felt good enough to begin training again. Then a new problem popped up. Her feet became very sore. **Blisters** appeared on the bottom of her feet. The skin peeled off in sheets. Soon her feet were so **swollen** that she could no longer run. She could hardly walk.

"What's wrong now?" she cried. Again doctors had trouble finding the answer. At last they decided the problem was the radiation. Somehow it was burning her feet. By this time, Gail's feet were a mess. They were in such bad shape that one doctor told her the feet might have to be **amputated**.

"You must stop walking at once!" this doctor ordered. "Stay off your feet until they **heal**! Two more days of walking on them and we won't be able to save them!"

## Will I Lose My Feet?

Gail was scared. She did what the doctor said. Her parents came to take care of her so she wouldn't have to walk. Every day her father carried her out to the porch to watch the sun set. She later said, "My biggest fear was, 'Will I walk again?' The last thing on my mind was, "Will I run again?"

Doctors stopped the radiation, and Gail started taking different medicine. Then she waited nervously to see if her feet would heal. Luckily,

Gail crosses the finish line just ahead of other runners.

they did. By April of 1991, her feet felt better. She was able to stand on them again. Soon she could **hobble** around wearing socks. By May, Gail was back in training.

**hobble**
walk slowly and with great difficulty

**progress**
movement toward a
goal

That summer she made great **progress**. She was happy to be back working with Coach Kersee. Every day she got stronger and faster. She still had to take medicine to control her thyroid. But for the first time in two years, she felt healthy and free from pain. In June, she won the U.S. 100-meter hurdle race. In September, she set a new American record for hurdles.

Gail said, "I feel I've been given a second chance. I've definitely had my share of bad times. But the road looks pretty good ahead of me."

## Crossing the Finish Line

In the summer of 1992, Gail Devers went to the Olympic Games. She hoped to win a gold medal in the 100-meter race. She knew it would be tough to do. Juliet Cuthbert from Jamaica would be hard to beat. So would Irina Privalova from Russia. Still, Gail thought she had a chance.

Arriving at the Olympics, Gail felt good. On the day before the race, however, her right leg became **numb**. She lost all feeling in it.

**numb**
lost feeling

"Oh, no!" she thought. "Not now!"

Gail talked to Kersee about it. "I probably need to have my thyroid medicine adjusted," she said. "But the race is tomorrow!"

Kersee asked Gail if she still had feeling in her arms. She told him she did. "Good," he said. "Then think about your arms when you run. Make your arms move fast and your legs will catch up."

Gail nodded. She didn't know if she could run that way, but she would try.

Gail got off to a good start in the race. As she flew down the track, she thought about what

Kersee had said. "Make your arms move fast. Your legs will catch up."

Nearing the finish line, Gail was right next to Cuthbert and Privalova. Two other runners were also right with her. Gail crossed the finish line, then looked around. No one knew who had won. Five runners had all finished the race within six one-hundredths of a second. It was the closest 100-meter race in the history of the Olympics. At last the winner was announced. Gail Devers heard Bob Kersee shout, "Yes!"

Gail ran toward him and jumped into his arms.

Then she began running around the track, waving to the crowd. As she did, she thought to herself, "A year ago, you couldn't walk. Now, you're running. You've just won the gold!"

Gail celebrating her 100-meter victory

# Vocabulary Skill Builder

## Part A

■ Write a paragraph using these three words from the story.

**swollen:** puffed up beyond something's usual size
**heal:** get healthy again
**progress:** movement toward a goal

_____

_____

_____

_____

_____

_____

_____

_____

_____

## Part B

■ Match each word with its meaning.

____ 1. hobble          a. cut off

____ 2. thyroid         b. a powerful kind of wave

____ 3. amputated       c. sore spots on the skin

____ 4. numb            d. walk with great difficulty

____ 5. energy          e. the power to do work

____ 6. blisters        f. without feeling

____ 7. radiation       g. the part of the body that controls how
                           fast food is burned

## Read and Remember

■ Answer the questions.

1. How did Gail do in the 1988 Olympics? _____

_____

2. How did Gail's thyroid problem affect her body? _____

_____

3. What did the radiation treatments do to Gail's feet? _____

_____

4. What did Bob Kersee tell Gail to do when her legs became numb?

_____

_____

5. What did Gail do when she learned she had won the 100-meter

   race? _____

_____

## Think and Apply—Finding the Sequence

■ Number the sentences to show the order in which things happened in the story. The first one is done for you.

____ Gail lined up at the starting line with Cuthbert and Privalova.

____ A doctor told Gail her feet might have to be amputated.

__1__ Doctors began giving Gail radiation treatments.

____ Gail's feet healed.

____ Gail Devers won a gold medal.

# 4x100 Relay Team

## The Perfect Race

**horror**
a feeling of fear and unhappiness

**stretcher**
a cloth-covered frame used to carry someone who has been hurt

**semifinals**
races that are run before the final race

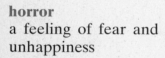

**relay**
a race between teams where each runner runs only part of the total distance

*U*.S. track coach Mel Rosen watched in **horror**. Mark Witherspoon was being carried off the track on a **stretcher**. Witherspoon was one of America's best runners. He had just hurt his leg.

Witherspoon's injury came in the 100-meter **semifinals** of the 1992 Olympics. It dashed his hopes of winning the gold in that race. It also meant he couldn't run in the 4 x 100-meter **relay**. Rosen had to find someone else. "It looks like Carl Lewis will get a chance after all," thought Rosen.

## Carl Lewis

Carl Lewis was no stranger to fans of the Olympics. Some people thought he was the best track and field athlete of all time. In the 1984 Olympics, he had won four gold medals. In 1988, he had won two more.

Lewis hoped to win more gold in 1992. But something happened that no one expected. Weak from being sick, he finished sixth in the 100-meter trial race. That meant he could not compete in that Olympic race. It also meant he wouldn't run on the 4 x 100-meter relay team. He would serve only as an **alternate** to the four runners.

**alternate**
someone who can take the place of a team member who is sick or hurt

Relay team celebrates their world record.

## A Second Chance
Carl Lewis soon **recovered** from the sickness that had **weakened** him. Just a few weeks after the trials, he beat Leroy Burrell and Mark

**recovered**
became healthy again

**weakened**
caused him to lose strength

Witherspoon. Both were members of the 4 x 100-meter relay team. But Lewis did not ask to be put on the team. He didn't want to bump one of the other runners. "They can win without me," he said.

Then Mark Witherspoon hurt his leg. Coach Rosen had to pick one of the alternates to take his place. Rosen called on Carl Lewis. He asked Lewis to run the last part of the race. This part is called the **anchor** leg. Over the years, Lewis had run the anchor leg on five world record relay teams. Now he would get one more chance. Right before the race, Lewis turned to teammates Mike Marsh, Leroy Burrell, and Dennis Mitchell. Lewis said, "Let's **dedicate** the race to Mark."

## Yes! Yes! Yes!

The Americans were favored to win the 4 x 100-meter relay. But anything could happen in a race like this. First one runner runs 100 meters. Then, while still running at top speed, he passes the **baton** to a second runner. The second runner runs his 100 meters. The baton is passed to the third, then the fourth runner. If someone drops the baton or doesn't make a good pass, the team will lose.

The Americans had not been passing the baton well. On the day of the race, they showed up at the track four hours early. Over and over, they handed the baton to each other.

Finally it was time for the race. Mike Marsh ran a smooth, fast first leg. He made a fine baton pass to Leroy Burrell. Burrell blazed through his 100 meters and made a clean pass to Dennis Mitchell. "When I saw Leroy coming," said Mitchell, "I knew we had a chance to break the world record."

**anchor**
last runner in a relay race

**dedicate**
do something in honor of someone else

**baton**
a small stick that relay runners carry and pass to each other

Lewis could see that things were going well. But the Cuban team was running right with them. "They're coming, Carl! They're coming," shouted Mitchell. "This is it!"

Lewis grabbed the baton and took off down the track. After just a few meters, he screamed out, "Yes! Yes! Yes!" He knew the other runners couldn't catch him. Lewis crossed the finish line in a new world record time of 37.40 seconds.

Carl Lewis crosses the finish line and sets a new record.

# Vocabulary Skill Builder

■ Complete the following sentences by writing the missing word in each space. Choose from the words in the box. When you are finished, the letters in the boxes will tell you one thing the 4 x 100 relay team did.

| semifinals | recovered | alternate | stretcher | horror |
|---|---|---|---|---|
| dedicate | anchor | weakened | baton | relay |

1. Witherspoon got hurt
   in the 100-meter ____ . __ __ __ __ __ __ __ __ □

2. Carl Lewis's sickness left
   him ____ . __ __ __ __ □ __ __ __

3. Witherspoon was carried off
   on a ____ . __ __ __ __ □ __ __ __

4. Dennis Mitchell passed Carl
   Lewis the ____ . __ □ __ __ __

5. As Witherspoon fell, Mel
   Rosen watched in ____ . __ __ __ □ __ __

6. The U.S. team won the
   4 x 100 ____ . __ □ __ __ __

7. Carl Lewis's leg of the race
   was called the ____ . __ __ □ __ __ __

8. Lewis was sick during the
   trials, but soon ____ . __ __ __ □ __ __ __ __

9. Carl Lewis was able to
   serve as the ____ . __ __ __ __ □ __ __

10. Lewis wanted to ____ the race
    to Mark Witherspoon. __ __ □ __ __ __ __

84

# Read and Remember

■ Some of the statements below are true. Others are false. Place a check in front of the three things that happened in the story.

_____ 1. Mark Witherspoon could not run in the 4 x 100 relay race because he hurt his leg.

_____ 2. Coach Rosen asked Carl Lewis to fill in for Mark Witherspoon in the 4 x 100 relay race.

_____ 3. Leroy Burrell dropped the baton as he tried to pass it to Dennis Mitchell.

_____ 4. A member of the Cuban team tried to trip Carl Lewis during the last leg of the race.

_____ 5. Carl Lewis had to drop out of the 4 x 100 relay race because a sickness had weakened him.

_____ 6. The U.S. men's 4 x 100 relay team set a new world record in the 1992 Olympics.

# Write Your Ideas

■ Pretend you are Mark Witherspoon. Write an entry in your journal. Describe your feelings as you watch your teammates win the gold medal in the 4 x 100 relay.

_____

_____

_____

_____

_____

_____

_____

# Glossary

**actually,** page 11
Actually means really.

**adopted,** page 37
To adopt is to bring a child into your family and raise him or her as your child.

**alternate,** page 81
An alternate is someone who can fill in for a team member who is hurt. The alternate only runs if a regular team member is not able to run.

**amazement,** page 68
Amazement is complete surprise.

**amputated,** page 74
To have something amputated is to have it cut off. Doctors may amputate diseased parts of a body to save a person's life.

**anchor,** page 82
An anchor is the last runner in a relay race.

**art,** page 54
Art is something that has beauty and special meaning.

**athletes,** page 3
Athletes are people who are trained in sports or other exercises. Swimmers, basketball players, and runners are athletes.

**attitude,** page 11
An attitude is a way of thinking about something.

**baton,** page 82
A baton is a small stick that relay runners carry and pass. The first runner passes the baton to the second runner who passes it to the third runner, and so on.

**blisters,** page 74
Blisters are sore spots on the skin that look like little bubbles.

**calm,** page 39
To be calm is to be relaxed and not excited or worried.

**captured,** page 47
To capture something is to win it.

**cast,** page 12
A cast is a hard plaster bandage that keeps broken bones from moving.

**championship,** page 6
A championship is a contest to see who is the best at something.

**combined,** page 17
When things are combined, they are mixed together.

**comeback,** page 68
A comeback is when a person leaves a sport, then returns to it and becomes good again.

**compete,** page 3
To compete is to try to beat others in a contest.

**competition,** page 28
A competition is a contest where a winner is chosen.

**confident,** page 12
To be confident is to believe in yourself and your abilities.

**content,** page 13
To be content is to be happy with the way things are.

**cranky,** page 13
Someone who is cranky is unhappy and a little angry. If you wake the baby up from her nap, she will be cranky.

**create,** page 47
To create something is to make something.

**crime,** page 58
A crime is an act that is against the law. Burglary is a serious crime.

**dazzled,** page 31
If someone is dazzled, he or she is amazed.

**dedicate,** page 82
If you dedicate something to someone, you are honoring that person.

**defeat,** page 24
A defeat is a loss in a contest.

**demanding,** page 53
Something that is demanding calls for a great deal of time and hard work.

**diet,** page 43
Your diet is the food that you eat. Panda bears have a diet of eucalyptus leaves.

**disappointment,** page 18
A person who is a disappointment, is someone who does not do as well as people expected.

**doubled,** page 24
To double over is to bend deeply at the stomach. When he heard the joke, he doubled over with laughter.

**education,** page 4
Education is the knowledge and training received at school.

**energy,** page 74
Energy is the power to do work. Your body turns food into energy, then uses the energy to work.

**expected,** page 66
If you expect something to happen, you think that it's likely it will happen. Ava expected to make all A's.

**express,** page 69
To express something is to put it into words.

**failure,** page 68
A failure is a loss or the act of not getting something you want. His failure to win a medal made him very sad.

**favorite,** page 67
The favorite in a race is the person who is believed to have the best chance of winning.

**fever,** page 38
You have a fever when your body is hotter than it should be. A fever is a sign of sickness.

**flunked,** page 6
To flunk out is to be kicked out of school because of failing grades.

**freestyle,** page 12
Freestyle is a kind of race where swimmers can move their arms and legs any way they want.

**future,** page 17
The future is the time yet to come.

**glory,** page 3
Glory is the honor and praise given to someone who has done a great thing.

**goal,** page 18
A goal is what a person is working toward. Her goal was to make the honor roll.

**grace,** page 44
Grace means moving your body in a smooth, beautiful way.

**growth,** page 44
Growth is the process of getting bigger. His parents measured his growth each year on a wall chart.

**gymnasts,** page 28
Gymnasts are people who jump and tumble. They use equipment such as the balance beam, uneven parallel bars, and the vaulting horse.

**heal,** page 74
To heal is to get healthy again.

**hobble,** page 75
To hobble is to walk slowly and with great difficulty.

**hockey,** page 38
Hockey is a game that skaters play on ice. The players try to hit a rubber disc with curved sticks.

**horror,** page 80
Horror is a feeling of great fear and unhappiness.

**hurdles,** page 61
Hurdles are a series of bars that runners jump over as part of a race.

**ignored,** page 24
To ignore something is to pay no attention to it.

**individual,** page 31
Individual means one single thing, not a group of things.

**infield,** page 62
The infield is the area inside a track.

**injury,** page 62
An injury is damage done to the body.

**instructor,** page 22
An instructor is someone who teaches or trains people.

**javelin,** page 61
A javelin is a long, pointed pole or spear that is thrown.

**margin,** page 25
A margin is the amount of difference between things. He won the race by a small margin.

**mastered,** page 54
To master something is to learn to do it well.

**medical,** page 4
Medical means having to do with medicine. Medical school is a school that teaches people how to be doctors.

**minor,** page 23
Something that is minor is small and not important.

**miracle,** page 45
A miracle is when something wonderful happens that cannot be explained.

**muscles,** page 68
Muscles are the parts of the body that give you strength and power.

**nervous,** page 28
To be nervous is to be jumpy and afraid instead of relaxed.

**numb,** page 76
Something that is numb has lost all feeling. My feet were numb after walking in the snow for an hour.

**officials,** page 19
Officials are the people in charge of something.

**peak,** page 10
Your peak is when you are the best you will ever be at something. Most gymnasts reach their peak during their teenage years.

**performance,** page 28
A performance is an act done in front of judges.

**platform,** page 34
A platform is a flat surface raised up off the ground. In the Olympics, some dives are done off a platform.

**poverty,** page 63
Poverty means having little or no money.

**predicted,** page 58
To predict is to make a guess about what will happen in the future. The weather report predicts snow for next week.

**prejudiced,** page 4
To be prejudiced is to think that certain groups of people are not as good as others.

**program,** page 53
A program is an act made up of certain moves and skills.

**progress,** page 76
Progress is movement toward a goal.

**radiation,** page 74
Radiation is a very powerful kind of wave. Radiation is sometimes used to burn a diseased part of the body in order to get rid of the disease.

**realize,** page 69
To realize a goal is to reach the goal and make it real.

**recovered,** page 81
To recover is to become healthy again.

**relay,** page 80
A relay is a race between teams where each team member runs only part of the total distance. A stick called a baton is passed from the first runner to the second runner, from the second runner to the third runner, and so on.

**reporters,** page 54
Reporters are people who write for newspapers and magazines.

**resort,** page 16
A resort is a place where people go to vacation. Every winter, the Miller family went to a resort on the coast of Spain.

**reverse,** page 35
To move in reverse, is to move backward.

**rink,** page 44
A rink is an area covered with ice for skating.

**risky,** page 36
Something that is risky is dangerous.

**rival,** page 18
A rival is someone who is trying to beat you in a contest or race.

**routine,** page 31
A routine is a set of exercises done in a certain order.

**scholarship,** page 61
A scholarship is money given to a student to help pay for school.

**scoreboard,** page 66
A scoreboard is a sign that shows athletes' scores in a contest or race.

**scraped,** page 29
To scrape is to rub against something.

**semifinals,** page 80

Semifinals are races run right before the final race. The winners of the semifinals get to run in the final race.

**senior,** page 52

Senior skaters are skaters who are at least eighteen years old. Seniors compete in different contests than junior skaters.

**shocked,** page 12

To be shocked is to be very surprised.

**shrugged,** page 22

To shrug is to move your shoulders up to show that you don't know something. When the teacher asked Mary what time it was, she shrugged.

**slalom,** page 18

A slalom is a race where skiers have to ski through gates that are set close together.

**somersault,** page 2

A somersault is a roll of the body where the feet go up over the head.

**springboard,** page 37

A springboard is a board that divers use to bounce high into the air when diving.

**stretcher,** page 80

A stretcher is a cloth-covered frame used to carry someone who has been hurt.

**stumbled,** page 54

To stumble is to trip and lose your balance.

**styles,** page 17

A style is a way of doing something.

**successful,** page 17

If you are successful at something, you are good at doing it. He was a successful student.

**suggested,** page 23

To suggest is to put forward an idea for someone else to think about.

**suspected,** page 43

To suspect is to think something might be true. The teacher suspected that Tom had cheated on the test.

**swollen,** page 74

Something that is swollen is puffed up beyond its usual size.

**syndrome,** page 42

A syndrome is a set of problems that makes up an illness.

**takeoffs,** page 47

A takeoff is the act of leaving the ice for a jump into the air.

**talent,** page 4

Talent is the ability to do something well.

**taxi,** page 25

A taxi is a car with a driver that you pay to take you somewhere.

**thyroid,** page 74

The thyroid is the part of the body that controls how fast food is burned.

**tragic,** page 12

Something that is tragic is very sad. Many people died in the tragic plane crash.

**trial,** page 38

A trial is a test. In the Olympics, trial dives are held to see who can be in the final competition to win a gold medal.

**triple,** page 53
Triple means three of something. A triple jump is a jump where the skater spins around in the air three times before landing.

**tucked,** page 37
To tuck is to curl into a ball.

**twirled,** page 50
To twirl is to spin around.

**uneven parallel bars,** page 29
The uneven parallel bars are two bars set side by side. One bar is higher than the other.

**vaulting,** page 29
Vaulting means jumping over a padded structure.

**victory,** page 25
Victory is the winning of a contest.

**violence,** page 58
Violence means using force to cause harm to someone. That city is known for its high rate of violence.

**volleyball,** page 61
Volleyball is a game where two teams of players use their hands to hit a ball back and forth over a net.

**vowed,** page 67
To vow is to make a promise.

**weakened,** page 81
Something that weakens you causes you to lose strength.

**worthwhile,** page 51
Something that is worthwhile is worth all the time and work put into it. He thought that band was a very worthwhile activity.

# Keeping Score

1. Count the number of correct answers you have for each activity.
2. Write these numbers in the boxes in the chart.
3. Ask your teacher to give you a score (maximum score 5) for Write Your Ideas.
4. Add up the numbers to get a final score.

| Stories | Vocabulary Skill Builder | Read and Remember | Think and Apply | Write Your Ideas | Score |
|---|---|---|---|---|---|
| Sammy Lee | | | | | /20 |
| Dawn Fraser | | | | | /20 |
| Jean-Claude Killy | | | | | /18 |
| Kip Keino | | | | | /20 |
| Olga Korbut | | | | | /15 |
| Greg Louganis | | | | | /20 |
| Scott Hamilton | | | | | /18 |
| Kristi Yamaguchi | | | | | /18 |
| Jackie Joyner-Kersee | | | | | /22 |
| Pablo Morales | | | | | /18 |
| Gail Devers | | | | | /20 |
| Relay Team | | | | | /18 |

# Answer Key

**Vocabulary Skill Builder**
  **Part A:** 1-g, 2-b, 3-f, 4-a, 5-c, 6-d, 7-e
  **Part B:** Answers will vary.
**Read and Remember**
1-b, 2-c, 3-a, 4-b, 5-b
**Think and Apply—Finding the Sequence** 2, 5, 4, 1, 3

**Vocabulary Skill Builder**
1. cast, 2. actually, 3. shocked,
4. content, 5. cranky, 6. peak,
7. freestyle, 8. attitude, 9. tragic,
10. confident. Code Word: Australian
**Read and Remember**
1-b, 2-a, 3-b, 4-a, 5-c
**Write Your Ideas** Answers will vary.

**Vocabulary Skill Builder**
*Across:* 1. disappointment,
5. combined, 6. rival, 7. goal, 8. slalom,
9. future *Down:* 2. successful,
3. officials, 4. styles, 6. resort
**Read and Remember** 1, 2, 6
**Think and Apply—Drawing Conclusions**
1. he skied so fast.
2. he wanted to learn from them.
3. he had done poorly.
4. they have trouble seeing the gates.
5. he won all three skiing events in the 1968 Olympics.

**Vocabulary Skill Builder**
  **Part A:** 1-c, 2-d, 3-a, 4-e, 5-b
  **Part B:** 1-a, 2-a, 3-c, 4-b, 5-c

**Read and Remember**
1. He entered the Police Training College.
2. He didn't have a coach.
3. He was having stomach problems.
4. He doubled over because of bad stomach pains.
5. His taxi got stuck in traffic.
**Write Your Ideas** Answers will vary.

**Vocabulary Skill Builder**
  **Part A:** 1. nervous, 2. performance,
      3. scraped, 4. uneven
      parallel bars, 5. individual
  **Part B:** 1-d, 2-b, 3-a, 4-e, 5-c
**Read and Remember** 4, 5, 6
**Think and Apply—Main Ideas** 1, 3

**Vocabulary Skill Builder**
*Across:* 2. trial, 4. platform,
6. reverse, 8. springboard, 9. tucked
*Down:* 1. calm, 3. adopted, 5. fever,
6. risky, 7. hockey
**Read and Remember**
1. The diver's head comes close to the diving board.
2. He scored a perfect ten at the Junior Olympics.
3. He did very well and won two gold medals.
4. He told Greg to do his last dives.
5. He said, "No matter what happens, my mother will still love me"
**Write Your Ideas** Answers will vary.

**Vocabulary Skill Builder**
1. captured, 2. suspected, 3. diet,
4. grace, 5. takeoffs, 6. create, 7. growth,
8. rink, 9. miracle, 10. syndrome
Code Words: A sick child

**Read and Remember** 2, 3, 5
**Think And Apply—Cause and Effect**
1. they were trying to find out what was wrong with him.
2. it was believed that exercise could help people with Schwachmann's syndrome.
3. they thought he would enjoy watching his sister skate.
4. he had lost six years of growth.
5. he wanted to make himself look taller than he really was.

| Kristi Yamaguchi | Pages 50-57 |

**Vocabulary Skill Builder**
  **Part A:** 1-g, 2-f, 3-b, 4-d, 5-a, 6-c, 7-e
  **Part B:** Answers will vary.
**Read and Remember**
1-c, 2-b, 3-a, 4-c, 5-b
**Write Your Ideas** Answers will vary.

| Jackie Joyner-Kersee | Pages 58-65 |

**Vocabulary Skill Builder**
  **Part A:** 1. crime, 2. volleyball,
        3. scholarship, 4. javelin,
        5. predicted
  **Part B:** 1-b, 2-c, 3-a, 4-b, 5-a
**Read and Remember**
1. The house had thin walls and tiny rooms and was in a bad neighborhood.
2. She dragged him out of bed so that he would get to track and field practice.
3. He told her she should be doing more track and field.
4. She began running faster.
5. She thought her greatest victory was escaping the crime and poverty of her early years.
**Think and Apply—Fact or Opinion?**
1-F, 2-O, 3-O, 4-F, 5-F, 6-O, 7-O

| Pablo Morales | Pages 66-71 |

**Vocabulary Skill Builder**
*Across:* 2. comeback, 6. vowed, 7. realize, 9. express 10. failure
*Down:* 1. favorite, 3. muscles, 4. amazement, 5. scoreboard, 8. expected
**Read and Remember**
1-a, 2-b, 3-c, 4-a, 5-b
**Write Your Ideas** Answers will vary.

| Gail Devers | Pages 72-79 |

**Vocabulary Skill Builder**
  **Part A:** Answers will vary.
  **Part B:** 1-d, 2-g, 3-a, 4-f, 5-e, 6-c, 7-b
**Read and Remember**
1. She did poorly.
2. She lost the sight in one eye, had trouble remembering things, and couldn't sleep at night.
3. The treatments burned her feet so badly she could not walk.
4. He told her to move her arms fast and her legs would catch up.
5. She jumped into Bob Kersee's arms, then ran around the track waving to the crowd.
**Think and Apply—Finding the Sequence** 4, 2, 1, 3, 5

| 4 x 100 Relay Team | Pages 80-85 |

**Vocabulary Skill Builder**
1. semifinals, 2. weakened, 3. stretcher, 4. baton, 5. horror, 6. relay, 7. anchor, 8. recovered, 9. alternate, 10. dedicate
Code Words: Set a record
**Read and Remember** 1, 2, 6
**Write Your Ideas** Answers will vary.